NETW(
PERSO

C000171258

By Zoe Bennett
Aka (Motivational Queen™)

MOTIVATIONAL QUEEN®

Networking Personified by Zoe Bennett

Copyright © 2017 Zoe Bennett

Chief Editor: Lee Caleca

Editor: Daniella Blechner

All internal content written and designed by Zoe Bennett.

Book cover design created by Lizzy Haynes of Innovation Creations Ltd.

All rights reserved. No part of this publication may be reproduced, stored in a retrieval system, or transmitted in any form or by any means, electronically, mechanically, photocopying, recording or otherwise without the prior permission of the publisher.

This book is sold subject to the condition that it shall not, by way of trade or otherwise, be circulated without the publisher's prior written consent in any form of binding cover other than that in which it is published and without similar condition including this condition being imposed on the subsequent purchaser. Whilst every care has been taken in preparation of this book, no responsibility for any loss occasioned to any person acting or refraining from any action as a result of any material in this publication can be accepted by the author or publisher or anyone else connected with the book.

First Printing 2017

Published by Conscious Dreams Publishing

www.consciousdreamspublishing.com

ISBN 978-1-9998091-4-0

CONTENTS

WHAT OTHER PEOPLE ARE SAYING ABOUT THIS BOOK

"Pages of networking wisdom and common sense. Essential reading."
Brad Burton Founder of 4Networking,
Author and the U.K's No1 Motivational Business Speaker

"Zoe is a fantastic networker, with the tips in this book, you can be too! Networking is a big part of business and everyday life, your network can be one of your best assets if you learn how to grow it and nurture it and use it to its full potential, the information in this book can help you do just that!"
Rebecca Dean, Company Director of Networking Group
Go 4 Gold Local Limited

"Networking Personified is an amazing networking manual and a 'go to guide' for anyone who wants to learn the art of effective networking. Written by the 'Networking Queen' Zoe Bennett, this interactive and practical book is a no-nonsense in-depth resource, whether you have years of experience in networking or are a beginner starting on your entrepreneurial journey. There is something in here for everyone, regardless of industry or expertise. This book will help you to demystify and gain clarity regarding the networking landscape, learn how to save time, add value to your business and increase sales and exposure for your brand."
Justice Williams MBE, multi-award winning entrepreneur,
inspiring people through the art of creativity and enterprise

"Yet another accomplishment alongside numerous others that this impressive and inspirational woman has achieved. Zoe is undoubtedly the "Queen of Networking" and calls on her vast networking experience to bring business owners this absolute goldmine of information that is a straight talking, straight to the point book which encapsulates the essence of networking. Not only does this book provide realistic effective examples, but it is superbly interactive in many parts. I would highly recommend this book to all, as networking is most definitely a part of everyday life no matter which path you travel."

Safaraz Ali, Social Investor, Entrepreneur and Head of Pathway Group

"Yet another accomplishment by this very motivated woman. Zoe Bennett just goes from strength to strength. Her success stems from her passion to help others and empower those that are less fortunate. She is very driven, very focussed and an absolute asset to have in your contact base.

She spends a lot of time networking, but networking to help others rather than for personal gain.

I would highly recommend this book as it will have the wealth of experience that Zoe has collected over the time."

Abid Khan, Senior Partner of Riverdale Insurance & National Director of Pathway2Grow

DEDICATION

I would like to dedicate this book to the greatest networker of all, my father, the late **Errol F Bennett**. He taught me so well how to engage effectively and sensitively to other people's wants, needs and desires. He showed me how to read people's energy levels and reciprocate accordingly. Understanding people was an art form to him which he nurtured and passed on to me over the many years. I am eternally grateful to him for making me more rounded, grounded, objective, and accepting of all people's situations and circumstances.

ACKNOWLEDGEMENTS

I would like to express my personal acknowledgement to **Linton Bennett** who has been my support system and without him I would not have had the time to network to deliver many gems of knowledge to you. **Paul Landa** M.D of Zeckro Web Solutions apart from being an expert in his field, he is one of the most kind-hearted people I have ever known and it is an honour to call him my networking partner in crime. He has a real genuine passion for helping others around him. I think everyone should have someone like him in their corner.

Daniella Blechner at Conscious Dreams Publishing, for being the last minute saviour.

Wendy Yorke, author coach and literary editor who restructured the content into balanced chapters.

Lee Caleca for editing the book and **Oksana Kosovan** for typesetting.

I thank you all.

INTRODUCTION

Before you begin

Before you begin reading this book, write down 10 words and 10 phrases that you associate with networking. This will be useful once you have done a 'compare and contrast' and revisit the terms after completing this book as it will demonstrate what you have learnt along the way.

Fill out this questionnaire beforehand, and then again at the end of the book, ideally after you have attended networking events and applied the principles. Tick the box that is most appropriate for you. Use two different colours, one for before and one for after, to see the comparison.

	Confident	Average	Daunted	Don't know
How do you feel about networking?				
How do you feel when meeting new people?				
How do you feel when initiating a conversation?				
How do you feel when delivering a pitch?				
How do you feel when referring others/finding referrals?				
How do you feel about 'excelling' when it comes to networking?				
How do you feel about asking for referrals?				

There have been a lot of twists and turns in my journey on the road that I call my life, and networking has been one useful tool that has positively helped me out in many different situations.

As a result, one day it came to me in a flash that I need to share what I know about networking and how it has worked out to be successful for me, bearing in mind that success is relative and unique to each person's interpretation. To quote Hector Urquhart, "One man's trash is another man's treasure". This reinforces that people view situations based on the model of the world they see through their own eyes; their experience of the world. This is called their *worldview* and it's based on everything that has ever happened to them, how it was resolved or ended and the people who interacted with them. It does not mean that they are right or wrong, but it is right for them based on their perception and perspective.

Through the chapters of this book, you will learn to make the networking process unique to you, your goals and your objectives as seen from a place of knowing what you want. Without a place of *knowing* there is no foundation upon which to build your valid opinions and measured individual plans.

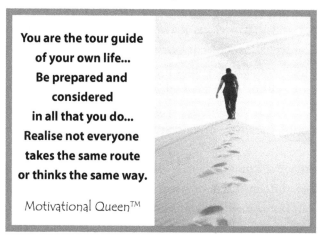

**You are the tour guide
of your own life...
Be prepared and
considered
in all that you do...
Realise not everyone
takes the same route
or thinks the same way.**

Motivational Queen™

The art of networking is all around us if we open our eyes and see all the amazing opportunities. But be under no illusion; **networking is not a one size fits all journey**.

In my case, it has been important to note that the initial *business element of networking* was not a part of my reality in the early days, my reality was purely *rapport networking*.

Rapport networking is where you naturally go out of your way to help another based on a humanistic urge and/or for the desire of building up a communicative relationship where you want to see the other person succeed. It can be a spoken or unspoken rapport as long as the underlying energy and interaction is that of trust and mutual understanding.

Over the years since my 'single figure age', time and time again I have been assisted, through networking, during adverse situations that have taken place in my life.

Networking appears in many forms and one of those forms is recommendations. Have you ever thought that networking is not always about finding someone to elevate your business or finding a client and that perhaps networking can be used for everyday practical scenarios too? For example, when there has been a need for a mechanic to fix your car and someone has recommended a person within your networking circle to help you solve the problem, *this* is networking; a time when there is a need to ask a connection for advice or guidance.

Now that we know that it is all around us, it is easy to have a mindset shift in terms of networking *not* being something that you join but something you signed up to the moment you were born. Your parents were not born with a parenting manual, but when they needed advice they would ask a connection, whether family, friend, colleague, or professional, as they did not know all the answers surrounding parenthood. The point I am making is **embrace networking positively, as it is inevitable and is always around you**.

I was never really conscious of the fact that any time I got into a difficult situation or I needed guidance or assistance with something, it was the art of networking that saw me through. It seemed I always knew a man that knew a man that knew a man who could assist me. This taught me that no matter what situation I got myself into, there was always a way out or a way around it. Luckily for me, that first person on my networking chain was my father. He was heavily connected as a community-spirited man and started Preston's first ever West Indian Community Social Club in my grandmother's living room with his friends. The real lesson here is to recognise that the person standing in front of you or the person you know directly may or may not hold the key to your solution. However, who they know or are connected to may just well be that all-important missing link.

The networking chain

Understanding the network chain is necessary so that your approach to networking will become clearer. This will make you less likely to be dismissive of the person you think is unable to help. They may not be able to solve the issue, but they just may be the person to connect you to or point you in the right direction of someone who can. No matter where you are in the chain, there is a link one way or another; you just have to look hard enough.

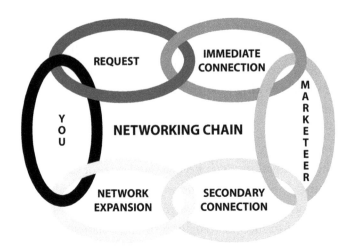

A chain is defined by the Cambridge English Dictionary as "a set of connected or related things". The networking chain it is not a conventional chain that goes in any particular direction. Every aspect is linked along the way. Each link above is connected in one way or another to form an everlasting chain. Each of the links will have at least two connections at any given time. Let's analyse each link in the chain.

You: You are at the centre of all networking. Whether you wish to connect to others or be connected by others. You are the common denominator. However, you could easily become a paid or unpaid marketeer for someone else within the chain. You always have that immediate connection whether it is someone that you have met at a business networking event or someone that you have built up rapport with in many different capacities. You will, over a course of time, inevitably have network expansion and create several secondary connections along the way.

Request: The request can be described as the underlying or transparent reason the connection exists in the first instance. It can also be described as the objective. This can be highlighted as the catalyst for any possible need or requirement for interaction. A request is needed before it can be facilitated as a referral to establish a connection. Without the request, there would be no reason to engage further.

Immediate Connection: The immediate connection (IC) is the first point of engagement, regardless of whether or not they can fulfill the request or go further down the chain and converse with the secondary connection. The IC processes the information given to them. They will have expanded their network through engagement with you as you will undoubtedly know people they do not know. This means that they can possibly connect you with the right people if you ask the *right* questions.

It is important to not only ask the right questions but to provide the right information (the more precise the better) to enable your IC to try and achieve the outcome you want.

Marketeer – If you are precise in your request and clearly translate what it is you require, then anyone you relay this information to potentially becomes your marketeer. They are your marketeer even in your absence. You will get the best results if you have been descriptive and left a positive impression for them to then promote you or your services when speaking to other people. Word of mouth is the most affordable and effective form of advertising. It is therefore important to have a great rapport and leave a long-lasting, positive impression.

Be clear about what you provide, your personal message (mission statement), your consistency, and your personal brand as this is what your marketeer will be referring to. You want it to be translated correctly so as to not disappoint the person it is relayed to. They will have expectations because of the information provided. How can someone market you if you do not have a clear message that can be easily replicated? It's important to work on this so you don't waste your opportunity to make a positive impact. Repeating what someone's objective is starts the chain for a marketeer as they will inevitability tell others about your aims and goals.

Secondary Connection – This is the person your immediate connection has connected with. This is also someone who is more accessible due to the proximity of the immediate connection. As the immediate connection knows them personally, they are more inclined to have faith in their recommendation or suggestion to connect with you and vice versa.

Network Expansion – The network expansion is the accessibility to connections beyond your immediate and secondary connections. Every time an interaction is made, there is an opportunity to expand your network. To make best use of the expansion, it is wise to have a clearly defined overview of who you are, what you do, what value you provide and who, if anyone, you would like to be connected to. Remember to keep it concise, precise and straight to the point, preferably within 30-60 seconds. Your network expansion builds your influence sphere.

We shall explore the practical nature of networking in this book and how to implement it according to Robert Kiyosaki's theory that "the richest people in the world look for and build networks; everyone else looks for work". We will see how true this is once you analyse your current methods and compare them with those that you will adopt and / or adapt with the guidance of this book.

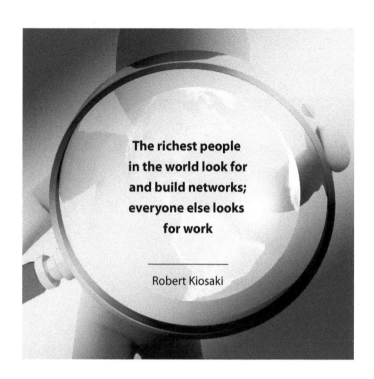

The richest people
in the world look for
and build networks;
everyone else looks
for work

———————

Robert Kiosaki

Chapter 1: What is Networking?

For many years, business networking has existed in different forms. However, it was not until a couple of decades ago that it became a lucrative industry to create some of the networking groups that exist today.

I derive from a background where people have always selflessly helped one another – *without* the need for a scheduled meeting, *without* regular 'meet fee payments', *without* a referral system, *without* the condition of only one person from each industry being invited and, most importantly, *without* paying for the service. The money of yesteryear was spent on the items or materials and not the time spent providing the service. This was called '**community**'.

It is because of this mindset, instilled during my upbringing, that my approach to networking is slightly different than the conventional method. It yields results, not always financial but in many other positive ways that you cannot put a price on such as great business connections that can help signpost or facilitate many of my requests. With such a strong network, I am able to connect people that would normally not have the chance to connect organically.

Build your connections

Networking is about building important connections to help elevate your business and professional stance. It is when you have built up a strong database that you are able to ensure being somewhat associated with whatever service or industry you are ultimately interested in. This approach may differ from person to person who enters the world of networking for the very first time.

Business owners network to build brand awareness, to generate business, to gain allies, to collect information about competitors, to increase the number of face to face interactions, to keep up to date with market trends, to discover innovative business ideas and, for some, it can even act as a final resort in keeping their business afloat.

You will not get
a second chance
to make
a first impression!

But you get
a second chance
to improve upon it!

Motivational Queen™

As we already know, 'word of mouth' is the most popular marketing tool and where networking is concerned, this could not be any more accurate. The need to create a long lasting **positive** impression can help facilitate such long-term, trusted relationships.

Networking is dependent on your mindset. Instead of asking the question, 'what can I get out of networking?' turn it on its head and ask yourself, 'what can I *put into* networking?'

It is normal to feel frustrated and discouraged if it initially seems as if you are not getting anything in return. Take a look back at the way you are approaching networking and your overall expectations. Bear in mind that networking requires patience, as it involves the development of long-lasting relationships and the steady expansion of your professional circle.

Who you associate yourself with determines how large a network you potentially expose yourself to and the differing types of people you will eventually have the opportunity to connect to. For example, being connected to 'Person A' could potentially open the door to their 3000 connections. Whereas, being connected to 'Person B' could possibly lead to 7200 connections, both direct and indirect. No matter how politically incorrect it may seem, people make judgments about the company you keep as it can reveal a lot about your character and aspirations.

Whilst remaining connected *within your* network, you can enhance your knowledge through your connections' expertise, experience and knowledge. It is imperative to have the mindset that recognises that the person you are directly networking with may not necessarily be your target audience on the surface, but their connections may be, so do not be eager to dismiss the person you are interfacing with.

Networking allows you to be more visible in front of an audience you may not have had access to previously. Unless you are 'out there', fewer people will know about you and your company. You may have the best attributes and personality in the world, but unless you are positioning yourself in front of an audience, then this cannot be translated.

The other point to note is that networking is not limited to face-to-face interactions, but also involves the incorporation of social media and identifying similar opportunities as they arise, or when you create them.

Networking most definitely is not limited to attending an event; it can happen whilst you are shopping, at the cinema, at a party, on an excursion; the circumstances are endless. Networking is about LISTENING for the key indicators and looking for opportunities, not just for yourself but for the other business people you are connected to as well.

Although actions speak louder than words use the words to guide you and listen to the message that comes from within the words.

Motivational Queen™

The true art of listening within networking is to keep a mental note of what you have heard, where you have heard it and from whom. You never know when it will become useful. For example, you could be in networking 'Group A' and someone vocalises to the room that they are looking for a juggler who can cover weddings based on a contract they have just secured to provide options for an entire entertainment wedding package. At this stage, you do not know anyone. You then go to networking 'Group B' and you hear a number of people stand up and say what they do, including a mobile child minder, a juggler, and an illusionist. Then you are out casually shopping and you overhear the cashier talking about her son who provides a venue dressing service. Then finally, you are at a friend's barbecue and he is showing a video that was filmed at his brother's wedding with an amazing singer that is a non-mutual friend.

Now that you're armed with this information, what would you do? You could fulfill the initial request and obtain the details of the juggler and make the referral or you could take it up a level and go above and beyond for many of the people you have interacted with by hearing not only that they wanted a juggler but that they had secured a contract to provide options for an ENTIRE entertainment wedding package. The opportunity exceeds expectations and provides your immediate connection with more than they requested, allowing them to have options.

The more people you refer to that person, the more likely that at least one will be the right fit for their company. You would connect them with the mobile child minder as they could offer a children's serviced area. The next would be to provide a further entertainment connection option by referring the illusionist from networking 'B' and the singer's details at the barbecue that you'd attended. Whilst shopping, you would ask for the details of the venue dresser only after you find out a little more about them. Pose questions. Is there somewhere you can view their work or testimonials? This gives you a reason to engage with the cashier who now becomes another connection – plus it helps you relay some background knowledge to your immediate connection to help with their decision-making.

The key is to continue to listen out for opportunities that could help the person who put out the original request and build upon your own connections at the same time through people engagement. This now helps you have a more extensive connection referral list that can come in handy at any given time.

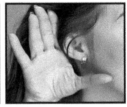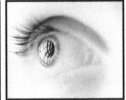

For some organisations, networking is more cost effective than traditional advertising, however, I see networking as a form of unconventional personal advertising; **people buy from people**. It is this mindset that helps with networking success.

The most important factors about networking are **KNOW, LIKE and TRUST**. People are not willing to do business with someone unless they first get to **know** about them, **like** what they say and, of course, **trust** that they will deliver.

You may point out that this contradicts how the majority of the nation sources services and goods. We naturally come from a culture where we simply turn to one of the popular directories, look up a number in a book, and make use of a service without the 'know-like-trust' element. However, this is not always the case; chances are that when you browse through a directory, you either see a brief synopsis of what the service provider does or there will be testimonials available as well as an indicator of whether they have a recognisable brand. All these elements reinforce the 'know-like-trust' model, meaning that you cannot escape from the KLT (Know Like Trust) model as this is an element of the entire process.

The CLEAR Networking Model

I prefer to take this one step further when approaching networking and ensure a higher success rate. I therefore use the "CLEAR" model (Consider, Listen, Engage, Approve, Refer). Networking needs to be made clear and make use of a concise strategy; putting this model into practice will provide you with the foundation of a useful action plan.

CLEAR Networking Model

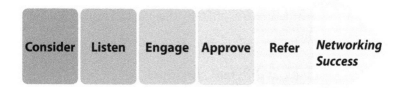

| Consider | Listen | Engage | Approve | Refer | *Networking Success* |

To start off with, you will need to **CONSIDER** *which* networking group you are interested in, *why* you want to attend their events and whether it 'makes sense' for you and your business. Once you are at your chosen networking event, it is important to **LISTEN** to the people in the room, look at their professions and seek conversation openings and any opportunities available for both them and yourself. As soon as you have heard that opening, you then must **ENGAGE** and remember that smiling is paramount as you want to be remembered for making a positive and long-lasting impression. After you have listened and engaged, you should decide whether or not you **APPROVE** of this person as someone you would like to do business with or feel good about referring. After assessing all the points, you can **REFER** that person comfortably.

Never refer someone that your gut does not take to as it is ultimately your reputation that is on the line. If you refer a 'bad egg', the lingering smell of your poor referral will be hard to shift.

By keeping the CLEAR model at the back of your mind, along with the other methods outlined in this book, your chances of success in business networking will be far greater.

Networking is more about you *as a person*, how you look at different situations, what you can offer, what you need, how comfortable you are interacting, how you look at opportunities, and how you come across as an individual. Let us explore each one of these insights.

• **How you look at different situations**

Start with first noting that very few networking interactions will be the same. They will differ slightly based on personalities, the setting and the objectives from either party or the mind frame each person is in. I have highlighted this so that you are open-minded with every interaction and know that some will yield visible positive results whereas others you may not see any positive results at all. I, on the other hand, see any networking interactions as yielding positive results because I am planting seeds of information every time. What you plant is entirely down to you and you alone. The more targeted information you provide about yourself, the more chance you have at succeeding within networking. I believe in making each interaction count with providing the best impression verbally and visually.

- **What you can offer**

You must ask yourself:

- What value do you provide to others?
- Why would someone want to engage with you?
- Why would someone want to have a one to one meeting with you?
- What would make someone want to possibly collaborate with you?

If you can articulate these before someone asks you, then you will be in a better prepared and more desirable position. It makes sense to give yourself that chance to make yourself intriguing and valuable to others and this is enhanced by being prepared for all those questions. Once you have defined your answers, utilize them in conversation as well as in your elevator pitch. The elevator pitch is when you have less than a minute to sum up who you are, what you do, why someone should engage with you, the value you offer and who you are looking for. The more precise you are, the easier it is for someone to understand what you have to offer.

- **What you need**

I have been to many networking events and also listened to informal networking interactions where the person has not said who they are looking for, meaning who is their ideal referral. It is important not only to say what you can offer but also to vocalize who you ideally would like to be connected to. Being specific will jog the other person's memory as to who they may know that can help facilitate this. Being specific could lead to many things such as gaining a contract, gaining a partnership or collaboration or extending your networking sphere for future use. The more precise you are, the easier it is for someone to respond positively and if need be help you gain those all-important connections.

- **How comfortable you feel when interacting**

If you behave in an awkward manner you make the other person feel uncomfortable. This is likened to mirroring. For example, if you smile the other person tends to smile, or if you tilt your head the other person tends to do the same and this is the same for coming across as awkward. You must be mindful of how you are coming across to the other person. If you are behaving in an awkward manner they may feel that you would be like that in a business interaction and may discount you based on that. If you naturally feel uncomfortable when networking, you must adopt techniques to relax you and to help with engaging more effortlessly. The quickest cost effective way is to practice and prepare by yourself. Practice in a mirror or record yourself and look at what other people will see and make subtle changes to help you relax and feel more at ease. Prepare template scripts for different interactions. This book will help you do all these things effectively.

- **How you look at opportunities**

It is paramount to look at networking as opportunities to build upon. How you analyse an interaction or outcome can change the direction in your mind as to the potential success of a networking opportunity. Some look at networking as wanting an immediate return on investment or results for the time spent networking, whereas others look at the long-term benefits. The benefits and validity of them are different for many people and it is therefore necessary for you to list the benefits that you can see or would like to see that would be beneficial for your goals. Some may not see the benefits whereas others see a correlation between the benefits of all engagement when networking. The defining level is to look at all interactions as a bonus and realize there is a lesson learned from all, but that lesson can only be seen from your perspective depending upon your objective. This reinforces that networking and the desired results are most definitely personal (personified) to each individual.

• How you come across, as an individual

Being mindful of how you come across is key. It is important to be self-aware of how you may come across to others – even if unintentionally. For example, you may be too pushy, too accommodating or perhaps your confidence can come across as egotistical. Be in tune with how you are portraying yourself as this can sometimes be misinterpreted by others. You want to try and find the right balance. Don't be afraid to deeply analyse yourself and remember to be completely honest and not critical of yourself. Many people engage based on what they initially see and whether it is pleasing to them and therefore it is important to remember to be objective more so than subjective. Other people silently assess and have a criteria such as:

• Is this someone I would want to refer?

• Is this someone I would want to do business with?

• Is this someone I want a business relationship with?

• Is this someone who can fulfill what they say they can?

• Is this someone who is what they say they are?

Plus many more qualifying questions someone silently asks themselves when determining whether to pursue the interaction. There are other benchmarks that people assess such as:-

• Does your brand complement or contradict itself?

• Is it authentic?

Get the above right or aligned and you will be in a better position when it comes to those all-important interactions.

Chapter 2: Why Do People Network?

The purpose of networking will differ from person to person and company to company. You need to establish what you are hoping to achieve by entering the world of networking. The cardinal sin that a lot of people initially make is to approach networking with the mindset of "what can I get from networking". I know many of you will be reading this thinking, 'but is that not the goal'? Let me break it down to you like this:

If you are a football player and have never met your team mates before, it can mean that you are on your own, trying to establish mutual relationships with others. You may say that your main objective is to score more goals than the opposing team and ultimately 'win' the match (your objective met). But, it is important to ask yourself, 'how do we get to become the winning team?', because it is not simply a case of entering a match and scoring goals – you need to first consider deciding where you want to play football, listening to the coach and taking heed of the other players' skills and techniques. You need to approve your trust in them and then refer the ball to them in order for it to travel up the pitch and have the opportunity to score.

Networking is no different. You do not approach it merely 'wanting some business', and expect it to just happen; it needs to be tackled methodically and worked around in a structured way – this will make the most of any opportunities at hand.

Networking opens a whole new world of 'face to face' as opposed to the faceless communications via telephone, email, or other methods. The various opportunities you will be exposed to through seemingly 'chance meetings', with new visitors and existing regulars in the room, immensely opens up your network. You might even get the opportunity to enquire about referrals from people in the room. Their connections may well help you get closer to that home run.

Many networking groups allow you to stand up and deliver a quick (approximately 1 minute) elevator pitch about you and your business. This not only makes your request more specific but gives other delegates the opportunity to refer you to a contact, and, of course, helps hone your public speaking skills.

Your network determines your net worth

Surround yourself with like-minded people who elevate and boost one another, as it is said that you become a product of the company you keep. People's mannerisms, attitudes, and all-round essence will rub off on you naturally. It is therefore important to gravitate and be around those who can draw out your creativity, innovation, drive, desire and knowledge, amongst many other attributes. Honest associates will provide you with constructive criticism, or guide you selflessly based on their experiences and out of the desire of wanting the best for you and your journey. Networking is a great opportunity to expand and strengthen your net worth.

Credibility

This is extremely important as it involves putting your money where your mouth is and standing up and telling people what it is you do and can offer. If you are unable to deliver, it will tarnish your reputation immensely as word of mouth is the biggest marketing tool. If word spreads that you did not or could not fulfill your role, it may well be detrimental to your business. Credibility means everything as you are ultimately hoping that someone will refer you in order for you to obtain further business, and this cannot happen if you have damaged your reputation.

The one thing that is guaranteed from networking, whether you are any good at it or not, is that your network will grow whether it's by one person or thousands. As soon as you interface with a person, that is when the networking ripple effect starts.

Networking ripple effect

The networking ripple effect is when you touch one person and that one touch multiplies by a hundred, and if you touch someone within that 100, it multiplies to a thousand, and it multiplies by itself over and over again until you potentially have accessibility to millions of connections. Being mindful of the possible connections that you could have access to helps you nurture every engagement and every interaction available to you. It is similar to telling yourself each time you are interfacing with someone that it is an 'indirect job interview' as people will silently be assessing what you say, how you say it, how you come across, and how you make them feel. Ensure that you are being the best, authentic version of yourself. In the same way that the ripple effect can expand, be conscious that it could easily start dissipating at any given time based on the way you are perceived by others. In light of this, always be that positive stand-out person that resonates in peoples' thought processes. Remember, sometimes you don't initially feel the ripple effect as it takes time to nurture and build up that all-important reputation that encourages others to connect you whether in your presence or not. Always be aware that you need to provide others with tools to help expand your network, such as an overview of what you do, who you are and the value you add.

Increase confidence and public speaking skills

Many business people are good at what they do, but when it comes to public speaking some are painfully shy, lost for words, freeze, or simply read word for word from a script. I have to categorically say that it is 'cringe-worthy' to watch somebody read from a piece of paper and explain to the room what they do on a day-to-day basis.

If you know your business, are a true expert and competent in what you do, then you should be able to talk about it as the passion and experience will shine through in your pitch. People buy into passion and the message becomes more vivid when they can see it flowing through your veins. Many people may never feel confident in doing business with someone who doesn't seem confident or knowledgeable about their supposed 'field of expertise'.

It is okay to write bullet points to help remind yourself of the order and not forget something crucial, but reading a script throughout your entire pitch does not cut it. If you need to or you feel that you cannot, then **practice, practice, practice** before you attend, as you will never get another chance to make that all important first impression. You do have the chance to redeem yourself during future meetings, but sometimes that first impression is everlasting and can cause you damage in the long run.

It is not completely unheard of to have had a business person deliver their pitch only for the room to still be unsure of what they do or how they could possibly refer them. It is crucial to keep things simple and specific and discuss each element of your business one at a time. Each should have a separate pitch in order to keep your audience on track.

The lesson here is to **be prepared**, to know your field, to talk about it confidently and know who it is you are asking the room to help you connect with. If you have to, create a fierce alter ego for your public appearances as this will help you push past that awkwardness or feeling of uncertainty about yourself. It helps to remember life is like a stage and it is how you play your role that will make the all-important difference. Note that although I am saying 'play it like you are on stage', you still need to stay authentic in what you are saying. You should be able to deliver what you say and ensure that you follow up with accuracy. This might sound like a complete contradiction, but, trust me, sometimes you have to fake your confidence to make it. It does not deter from the fact you still need to do what you say you can do as that is something you cannot fake long-term.

Maintain what you can sustain. As I said earlier, your credibility is always on the line and it only takes one act of untruthfulness to bring it all tumbling down. People tend to overlook the power of looking someone square in the eye when talking. If you can see the whites of somebody's eyes it is said that they are more than likely trustworthy, but don't confuse this with staring into their eyes like a deranged person. Ensure that when you are in conversation, you do not seem preoccupied or have something else on your mind or that your eyes are darting around the room. These are all signs of disinterest. Even if you feel that the person in front of you is not very interested in you and your needs, be mindful that you do not know about their acquaintances; for all you know your perfect referral could be in their contact chain. You need to find the right balance of holding a gaze and holding it with a sincere smile and an 'air of interest' as you do this. You are likely to receive more interaction from an audience if you seem genuinely interested in them; your facial expressions will give a lot away so be very wary of how you are coming across as this could either attract or repel certain individuals.

Motivate Yourself

You need to be disciplined to stay the course with business networking as many people, due to varying personal experiences, find their perception of instant financial gain does not materialise when they would like. It is about having the dedication and patience to give it time. There is no guarantee financial reward will come, but there are many other valuable benefits that networking can yield such as strategic partnerships, trusted connections or trading of services and/or products (where money is not exchanged but a business need is fulfilled). There are many non-financial benefits that, if the service or product had been monetised, would have saved a business money. This is where mindset comes to the forefront again. Understand that an actual exchange of money is only one way for you or your company to benefit yourself or others.

Believing in oneself and the underlying reason that you are networking should never be out of sight. A feeling of no gain can creep in, but being mindful of your objective should be a priority. The more you believe and know that your product and service is required, the more successful you will be, however, the success is attributed to your delivery. If you are seen as not having confidence or being motivated by your offering, how can anyone else be?

Having enthusiasm and sharing that becomes infectious in your surroundings and the people you engage with. Having a positive outlook over every conversation, over every scenario, and relaying that through your body language, through words and through your aura will encapsulate people. Make people feel that they want what you have in terms of your upbeat nature where you show that nothing fazes you and there is always a solution and an upside to everything.

There will be times where challenges will come your way and people are watching, people are lurking and people are silently assessing your behaviour, your reaction and your resilience. Networking tests your personal development as you will come into contact with many differing characters, differing requests, differing positives, and differing obstacles. Don't be afraid to self-reflect every day as this will help you be the best networker that you personally can be in line with your aims, objectives and your goals.

Create a self-reflection diary and use it to enhance your daily interactions as well as your continuing personal development.

Self-reflection diary

Date	Affirmation	Self Reflection	Future Amendment	Congratulate

Date	Affirmation	Self Reflection	Future Amendment	Congratulate

Each evening before you go to bed, write in your self-reflection diary anything you could do better going forward. Think about how you would deal with that situation based on any new experiences you have acquired.

It is important that you list the self-reflection first before you go on to the next step, as the last thoughts you have at night tend to stay with you whilst you sleep. For example, if you have a 'to do' list and you are worrying about fulfilling it the next day, you will likely have an unsettled sleep with this task at the forefront. The purpose of the diary is to get it out of your head; to put it where you can see it. Your perspective of those thoughts will change when they hit paper as you are analysing and assessing them methodically and with more clarity.

When they are put on paper, some of the thoughts become insignificant or they become more of a priority than others. Locate the hierarchy of thoughts and dissect them. There are no rules for length of time you spend with your diary but the more attention and time you spend reflecting and adjusting, the easier it will be to input, absorb and create positive thoughts and these will be the last thoughts in your mind before you fall into a restful sleep.

The positive insertions you want to enter into your thoughts are that of self-congratulation. Congratulate yourself for an achievement you gained that day, no matter big or small. It could be as simple as keeping your weekly planner up to date as this shows you were being mindful throughout your day, or it could be as big as winning a contract. It is irrelevant how substantial it is as the real victory is in implanting positivity about yourself that will naturally emulate to others when you are in their presence or conversing with them.

Now that you have self-reflected and congratulated yourself, you must boost yourself with affirmations, as the more you say them the more they become your reality. There are skeptics out there that don't believe affirmations work, likely because they have never tried them, don't understand them or don't want to put in the work.

All affirmations are subjective and unique to each individual; you have to find one that works for you, not one that works for others. They can be anything you need them to be, but they will only work if you join mind, body and spirit in your belief in your own affirmations. You must wholeheartedly believe in the words you are using.

My affirmations are "I can", "I will", "today is my day", and "I am awesome". However, I don't say them as if I am having a normal conversation. I say them with gusto, with fire in my belly because I believe every single word I am saying and that reflects outward each day in my interactions with others. What I'm putting in reflects and goes back out; in other words, the reflection of me represents how I feel about myself. Not only does this lift my personal confidence, it impacts my surroundings and the people within my sphere who see and feel the positive energy of my inert passion. It also has an incredible snowball effect. The more positive energy I put in and reflect out, the more positivity I attract and create around me.

So, my personal interpretation of I am awesome translates as:

Say your mantra several times. Once you start this, you will get pumped and guess what? You'll find, as I did, that **it works**. I believe in this so strongly it led to my trademarked name, the Motivational Queen™.

I AM
AWESOME!!!

If you struggle with saying the words, use post-it notes and put them in the areas you frequent most. You can put them in your personal space such as bathroom mirror, inside wardrobe doors and fridge, desk or computer monitor, etc.; learn to be inventive and it becomes fun. Have it in the car mirror above your head so when you open it you can see it instantly. It's there to remind you and reinforce what you want to emit to the people in your environment. It is okay to have statements as well as buzzwords such as *I am awesome, believe in yourself, I am a person of worth, I will succeed.* Buzzwords are used to give you that positive feeling of adrenaline. It is important to tell yourself these words or phrases and not wait for validation from elsewhere. Ultimately, you need to be able to tap into this at any time. It should become a natural way of existence, one that positively enhances your networking interactions and experience.

Chapter 3: Networking Mindset

I have said time and time again that it is not about asking what you can get out of networking as the leading factor, but of saying what can you put into networking. This is no more difficult than ensuring your mindset is positively aligned. Knowing that every interaction causes a reaction albeit negative or positive, it's important to understand that you don't need to be perfect. It takes many people years to master and, of course, learning varies with each individual. But know that learning from mistakes is as much a part of the process as any other component.

How you learn from your mistakes, however, is what will set you apart from your counterparts. The only way to get on in life and achieve is to continually and silently self-analyse your behaviour. If you don't like to be spoken to in a particular manner, ensure you remind yourself not to speak to others that way. If you don't like waiting for others, do not let others wait for you. This is the principle basis of "do unto others as you would have them do unto you". This should constantly play in your head on a daily basis and should be the foundation of your personal and business life.

The quickest way to be conscious of this is to shout to yourself in your head each day "reflection, reflection, reflection". What I mean by this is that every action you do in any given day should be reflected upon. Were you happy with how you approached each situation of your day?

If the answer is yes then you either have been conscious of your behaviour through constant reflection or you are too stubborn and single-minded to care or notice your failings.

If the answer is no then you are being honest with yourself and this is the first step to being a better rounded conscientious person that others will be proud to have in their network expansion.

The key to making the necessary mind shift is to look at every engagement as positive; an opportunity for a lesson learnt if you look hard enough to see it. For example, if you did not come across the way you wanted to in your elevator pitch, then this has provided you with an opportunity to reflect and rectify it for the next time and the time after that. If you felt that someone did not engage with you the way you would have liked, instead of being upset or dismissive of them the next time, use it as fuel to work harder to engage on your terms. This could be as simple as asking the right questions to draw their attention and soften their demeanour. After all, you have to remind yourself they are there to network also and they may not be ready, holistically, in their approach to be able to see beyond what is in front of them.

The experience with them will make you more aware of the signs to look out for and to ensure you have a contingency plan in place with those all-important introduction and conversation-saver questions (we will look at these further in the book). They may be a product of networking stereotypes that the more analytical and considered networkers see beyond. Do not spend too much time worrying about their mindset, but focus on yours as ultimately you are there for a particular goal and you do not want anyone interfering with that.

Get over yourself

Get over yourself! It is as plain and simple as that when it comes to feeling comfortable in the room.

You are at a networking event for a reason, so do not let yourself get in your own way of developing important business connections. Do not just stand there like a wet lettuce expecting others to approach you. It is more than likely that you will be waiting a long time and the lost puppy look will no doubt show and put others off. You have to exude an air of confidence to encourage others to feel the need to find out more about you.

Please do not confuse confidence with arrogance. I have seen a networker say to someone that they did not want to talk to them because they are an MLM (Multi Level Marketeer) and have no use for their services; THIS IS RUDE! Take the time out to listen to everyone; as surprising as it sounds most MLM's have a second, third, or sometimes even fourth job which in turn yields a number of diverse connections that you could miss out on simply by being judgmental.

A cardinal sin is to have your back to the room, particularly to someone that is trying to get involved and have a conversation.

I know of networkers who arrive at the venue far earlier than others to ensure that they are the first people in the room. This eliminates the daunting 'awkwardness' of walking into a jam-packed room and trying to participate in ongoing conversations with other professionals.

Strategic planning

When you decide to use networking as one of the tools to accumulate more business, it needs to be carried out in a methodical and strategic manner. Thinking that you will turn up to a networking event and see 'what will happen' is one approach but not necessarily the best approach.

- Firstly, think about the distance you are travelling; is that area your ideal demographic or would you want it to be a new market?

- Secondly, is it a yearly membership subscription group with attended meeting fees in addition or is it only the meeting fee that is payable; what can you afford and what can you sustain if you feel after the first meeting it is a group you want to visit regularly?

- Thirdly, are you prepared to be engaging and have a clearly defined message that briefly explains your business, what you can offer and most importantly how people can refer you?

- And finally, do you have the commitment, if the group is a fit, to regularly attend to, build and establish those all-important relationships?

All these questions need to be answered before you attempt networking in order to have a greater chance of success.

DON'T BE HASTY!

I have crossed paths with individuals who are too hasty, far too many times, as they do not consider what a group can offer in correlation for their business. It is not a quick fix initiative to just turn up to a networking group, expecting to feel at home and get instant referrals. Like with anything in business, it is paramount to do your due diligence. This is only achieved through extensive research.

RESEARCH, RESEARCH, RESEARCH!

My tip to anyone thinking about networking is to be a visitor at least twice before committing or deciding about any particular group. You need to get a feel of the room as the first time will likely always be different than subsequent visits. By visiting a group at least a couple of times beforehand, the common 'ambitious expectation' will more than likely become balanced out. Never just take anyone else's word about a networking group being good or bad, as it is solely down to your experience, goals and personal attitude towards networking.

Gaining value from networking does not always have to be in the form of money. Think about the benefits of adding names to your email list, valuable testimonials, discounts for (and from) connections and sometimes contra deals. A contra deal is where you are trading your skills, products and or services with that of another person's with a mutual understanding that money is not the trading tender. You can call it bartering.

We recognise the important linkage between a business and networking by asking ourselves why we are networking and how it will benefit our business. The answer to these questions should be that it is simply another marketing technique that is expected to yield a return like any other marketing activity.

For example, if we position ourselves in a particular magazine that does not have the right demographics for our business, the success rate or return on investment will be low. It's the same in networking.

Most business people have a business plan in which an overview of intended 'marketing' will be included. Networking is also a form of marketing and should be treated in this way. It is a good idea to set a budget aside for marketing and, in turn, ensure that a portion of it is used solely for networking. This will eliminate any surprises when you look over your business expenditures and help allay feelings of resentment on the amount of money you may spend on networking.

Strategic partnerships are another way to tactically plan within networking. Some call it synergy where some describe it as establishing partnerships and collaborations. Once you come across individuals who share similar business goals as yourself (*even if they are in the same field*), there is always room for synergy. Opportunities for collaboration will only become clear after a face to face business meeting, where you will be able to discuss ideas that are mutually beneficial. If done right, networking can grow your business, and using business collaborations is one of the many methods that will help you expand your reach.

Look at networking as branding

Your appearance and approach to networking will determine your success. You need to be aware of how your image reflects upon your business and the perception others have of you. This is why you have to look at the branding element of networking; your personal and business branding are fundamental; branding should be one of the foundational elements of your business. Branding is a part of planning and a method of advertising, it will make you stand out from the crowd and make you memorable, hopefully in a good way.

There are many ways you can create *brand awareness* (helping others notice your brand and associate it with you and your company) when you are in a room with other networkers, including:

- wearing a company logo on your clothing;
- wearing a distinct colour scheme, each time you are representing your company;
- owning a garment that is representative of you and your brand, like a yellow scarf or tie;
- bringing along an item that represents your company like a show-and-tell prop;
- using a pull up banner;
- using the closing punch line that you say at the end of your pitch (and make sure you say it, every time).

There are significant ways to draw people in so that they'll want to remember your brand.

- Simply be approachable.
- Be known for successfully connecting other business people.
- Be yourself: a gregarious 'larger than life' character if this suits you or a philanthropist or humanitarian if this suits you.

Branding only works when a *brand* is used consistently. Being consistent with your branding will reinforce consumer awareness; but in the case of networking, it's your approach and personality coupled with your positivity that will encourage people to come back, thus creating brand loyalty.

The key is that every time you use one or several of the above methods, you reinforce your brand. Do this enough times and it will be instantly recognisable. Your message – the one associated with your brand – will travel directly to your audience.

Ideally, you should reach the point that even when you are not in the room, people will still be talking about you and your individual, specific stand-out image. The moment you choose to break free from your image, you will confuse and disappoint your prospective audience. Your brand and maybe even your personal character will now be in question. If you don't believe in your brand and its significance, you will be unable to convince your target market of its value.

If you are a lone worker, this is even more important. You do not have the luxury of having a down day and letting someone else in the company push the branding. You essentially become the brand of the business whether you have a fancy logo, a fancy website or great marketing literature. Ultimately, when it comes to that all-important face-to-face interaction, you have to make a positive impression and hopefully secure that business deal.

You might argue that it is also *what you know* that will determine the strength of your brand and that is true to a small extent, but it is no good if you are socially inept and leave a negative interpersonal approach in the mind of your prospective client. In addition, branding is not about *what* you know it is about *how well* you can create the image you want to project and spark a person's interest. It is about making your philosophy and services clear to anybody who sees that image for the first time.

Your branding and how you conduct yourself is a representation of you and your business; not only face-to-face but on social media. Sometimes you do not get a chance to initially meet your contact face to face. You may not get to meet them personally at all, but you will meet each other virtually. What I mean by this is that many people nowadays perform an online search to find out about you. Have you ever Googled yourself? If you have not then maybe it is time that you did to give yourself a heads up as to what others see when they search for you. If it is favourable you can reinforce this with them and if it is not favourable then at least you can prepare yourself to disperse what is posted or look for ways to create new content to push it down the search list.

People will always be on the lookout for consistency between what you say your brand represents and your actual actions. If you are a make-up artist you cannot say you are the best in the game or that you can make people look a million dollars if you yourself look like a bag of wilted spuds. Think about the way you communicate; how you draft emails reflects your quality of work. Even how you dress is extremely important (as well as your personal hygiene!).

The message here is take the time to really think about how you want your image to be perceived and what you can realistically deliver when it comes to complementing your branding.

Chapter 4: Visibility Top Tips and Your Elevator Pitch

"How you project your image is how people will perceive you"
The Motivational Queen™

Project your image

Be consistent

Do not only say who you are but embody it. Avoid contradicting your brand.

Be visible and accessible

Turn up to networking meetings and attend events. Have an easy way for people to get in touch with you.

Create your story

Give the audience a reason to want to know more about you.

Create a mailing list

However, use it only for updates and providing relevant information. Do not inundate your contacts with email marketing; keep it relevant.

Offer something for free

For example, free advice, your expert knowledge, an eBook, a vlog, blog, etc.

Join online community sites

Constructively contribute often.

Create regular content

The content must reflect you well and encompass your field of expertise. Don't keep this in a content graveyard where you create the content and never distribute it.

Guest speak

Guest speak as often as you can about your field of expertise, collecting your visible proof each time to create your portfolio of evidence in the form of written or video testimonials, pictures, video clips, media articles, etc.

Become the 'go to' person

Overly understand your field of expertise.

Create your own mission statement

Include your values and stay true to them when being visible.

Promote others

Wherever possible recommend and connect people. Don't just talk about the value you offer, also vocalize the value others in your networking sphere offer as long as it is not a conflict of interest.

Show passion to your audience

Relay through your upbeat positive interaction how important what you say and how you say it is to you and ultimately others.

Engage with as many people as possible

Do not niche yourself out of markets; build relationships.

Obtain media coverage

Put out press releases and try and establish relationships with the media.

Attitude

TOP TIP ALERT

Ask yourself what you can *put into* networking *not* just what you can get out of it. As selfless as this may sound it is the only way to obtain the desired results you are after. If you approach networking in a selfish, self-absorbed, self-indulgent manner, it will no doubt become evident to the other people you are interacting with. This attitude will more than likely repel people, give you a bad reputation or put you on their radar of the people to consciously avoid. The funny thing is if you point out this behaviour to the ones that do it, many will swear blind that they are 'not guilty'. However, the smart ones will adjust their behaviour and recognise that what you are saying is a result of your constructive observations. It is easier to take that advice from someone that practices what they preach.

Be aware of the successful networkers and business people around you, and if they offer you advice, act humble and wise enough to absorb it in the manner that's intended. Stubbornness is the sure-fire way to halt your personal development and business growth.

Always take advice when it comes to receiving constructive criticism with regards to the way your message is relayed to the rest of the room. If your pitch is simply not working, do not keep hashing it out and regurgitating it during every meeting. Look at ways to improve it or restructure it in order to get the right conducive message across. Below is an example of what should go into your elevator pitch.

Elevator pitch

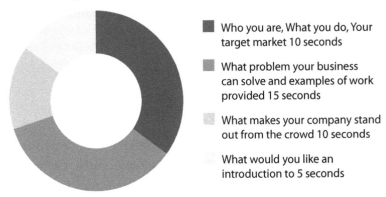

- Who you are, What you do, Your target market 10 seconds
- What problem your business can solve and examples of work provided 15 seconds
- What makes your company stand out from the crowd 10 seconds
- What would you like an introduction to 5 seconds

If you cannot fit the above points into 40-60 seconds then practice ways to make it happen, remembering that less is more. What I mean by this is if you are multi-faceted, do not talk about an arm's list of things that you offer; focus on one or two each time you are networking or relaying what it is you do. It is possible to overload people with too much information; they will not be able to process it effectively.

It is okay to have many bows to your string, but streamline it for every time you present your elevator pitch. I like to change my elevator pitch so that it is as relevant as possible for the audience. If I have spoken in front of them several times, instead of repeating the same content, I tell them a new interesting fact that they

5._____

_____

6._____

_____

7._____

_____

Use this as a way to sell/promote yourself by reiterating the positive 'buzz words' that other people use to describe you.

Write down who your ideal client is and why

_____

_____

_____

_____

_____

_____

_____

_____

_____

_____

Incorporate this into your elevator pitch towards the end

Show up and be present

It is important to show up and be in the present moment otherwise you are wasting valuable time that you could be using more productively and effectively elsewhere. It is simply not enough to just turn up to a networking meeting; you should be interested and, in turn, be interesting.

- Be interested in finding out about the people that you are networking with.
- Go out of your way to approach people.
- Don't plant yourself firmly expecting other people to approach you.
- Think long and hard how you would like to be treated and then "do it".
- Get out there and introduce yourself.

If you are nervous or unsure of what to say then practice, practice, practice and prepare and *prepare* beforehand. There are many ways you can practice and prepare. You can:

- create a script for yourself with different eventualities (detailed later in the book);
- try recording yourself;
- practice in front of the mirror or in front of another person you feel comfortable around.

Keep at it as the more you do this, the more relaxed you will feel when it comes to the real-life presentation. Don't forget to think about those faithful prepared 'go-to' questions that you can use at the right moment; the questions that have been useful to you time and time again in the past.

It is wise to try and delight people with the knowledge you have about them or what they do. If you know a particular company is going to be in attendance of an event and you would like to build a business relationship with them, do your homework. Learn as much as you can about them in the time you have. Know who their senior officers are, their marketing venues, their structure and anything else that might help you gain plus points and break down those daunting barriers quickly. By researching your potential leads, you will give yourself 'an edge'. Paying attention to what has been said and being able to repeat elements such as their name correctly or a small detail helps to build rapport. Being personable but not personally intrusive is what is required to strengthen the conversation.

Utilise the Engagement Rule where you make reference to the other person or ask them questions 3 times before you provide information about yourself.

Engagement Rule

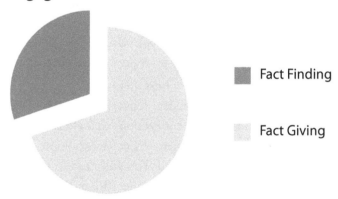

Fact Finding

Fact Giving

This may seem unbalanced but it is effective. It puts people at ease when they do not feel on the end of an onslaught of pushiness and perceived agenda ticking.

• Be interesting but not self-absorbed where the conversation is one sided, or as I like to call it, a "buy my stuff" conversation. This is where the conversation is dominated by a hard sell conversation all about the seller and what product or service they are trying to pitch.

- Do not overload your associate with too much information as you must remember they are there to interact with several people and are likely to be carrying a barrage of information already.

- If it is a one-to-one setting, you want them to have the most interesting information about you, but if you provide them with too much of this, they will only remember selective facts (as deemed appropriate by them). This will not work in your favour, as they may not have picked up on the most engaging points about you. Be mindful of *what* and *how much* you say and whether it is relevant or not in relation to the message you want translated.

- Educate people about what you do instead of selling to them as this will help them understand your services and proposition better. This can be in the form of relaying testimonials that you have received or reiterating any stories you have encountered in the course of your work to help people visualise what you do and how other people have found your product/services useful.

- You must also make a point whilst networking to vocalise whom it is that would be your ideal referral. Again, this helps others narrow down the list of connections that come to mind much faster and concisely. Be prepared to say who you would like to be connected to when asked. You will need to question your own marketing strategy if you are still not completely clear about this. If you answer, "I would like to be connected to anybody and everybody," then you are marketing to no-one.

- Another way to be interesting is to find a common ground and then use this as an initial ice-breaker until you feel that you are both at ease.

- If you have an interesting back story in relation to how you found yourself or positioned yourself in your current business situation it is advisable to share it, but not draw it out. Pick out the most interesting hooks within your journey. Many people like to know the person behind the brand or behind the business exterior.

Synergy not competition

I once came across a lady whilst networking who professed that she was the 'best in the game' and, don't get me wrong, she was good and very well connected, but her attitude towards somebody excelling beyond her in networking was far from perfect. Sadly, she celebrated other people's successes only if they were in a different field. Instead of embracing the successes of others in her field, she let them eat away at her and became upset at the thought of somebody else excelling in areas that she wanted to dominate.

The reason that the 'successful person' in this encounter was able to achieve their goals was because the seemingly self-absorbed networker would throw her dummy out of the pram and withdraw her support, thinking that she could pull the strings and leave the other person high and dry, expecting them to grovel for her not to retreat. Whereas the other person was resourceful and found other ways to challenge this woman's erratic behaviour. We can almost sympathise with her as she missed out on further valuable contacts as well as the contacts the successful person would have assisted her with, all because of her self-destructive approach.

Now, if I was able to identify such a disappointing demeanour, then I'm sure that others in her networking circle did as well. However, despite all the negativity, the successful person chose to give the erratic lady a chance and gave her information about a couple of fruitful leads that led to her generating business. Even after this, this poor networker did not show gratitude and continued with her unappealing behaviour towards the other person.

The lesson learned here is to keep away from self-destructive people as they can draw you into their negativity and consume you with their issues. It is advisable to focus on synergy as opposed to competition, but if you come across a difficult person like the one I crossed paths with, then be fully aware of the defective impact they can have on your mindset and your business; STEER CLEAR!

When it comes to meeting like-minded people who are from the same field as you, it is normal to feel initially 'put off' or even threatened. However, you may be surprised. On the surface, it may seem as if you do the same thing, but in fact you may just be offering something that is simply similar. Bear in mind that this allows you both to fill in the gaps for each other's business and create a stronger unified image for your prospective clients. Strategic synergy may also open the door to more clients who may have been unattainable BEFORE. Now that you have an extended network, they are finally within your reach.

Be smart, collect knowledge

You can attain a wealth of knowledge from networking groups by tapping into the minds of other established business people. They can even serve to be a consensus about you and your business and help give you guidance and direction. You see, many people hire a business coach to give them that all important "kick up the backside and focus" within their business, but if **you** are a smart networker, you will tap into the accomplished successful people in the room and seek their take on how they feel you could drive your business forward successfully.

Chapter 5: The Misconceptions of Networking

One of the main misconceptions of networking is that it is an avenue to generating business sales. It is this, plus much much more. Generating business is an element of networking, but gaining more knowledge, building your network, looking for synergy and keeping yourself informed about the current market trends and relevancy to the world is what real **networking** is about. A good network encourages you to excel beyond your wildest dreams, to look for new opportunities, to make you feel like anything is possible if you apply yourself. Furthermore, it helps you fulfil your goals with the connections you make, utilise their skills, hone your own skills, and share their contacts with your inner circle.

There are several other misconceptions about networking detailed below.

- **Networking usually costs a lot of money**

Another common misconception is that networking has to cost a lot of money. This is simply not true as there are several free membership networking groups out there, if you look hard enough. There are also free membership groups that do not have a meeting fee either. Networking will cost as much as you are willing to invest into it. Remember, the key word here is INVESTMENT. You must look at networking as an investment and not a 'bolt on'.

Try not to assume that it just takes up too much time that you would rather be spending in your business. Networking should be part of your marketing strategy and therefore is *not* taking time away from your business. It should be looked at as another valuable arm for it.

• You only succeed if you are in a clique

You can choose to let this hinder you or be prepared to get involved by approaching people first and interacting. Do not look at it as a clique but as formed relationships. A 'clique mentality' creates a barrier of people who are not willing to let someone in.

• You will end up standing on your own for most part of it

This will only happen if you do not actively engage and make the step to introduce yourself and get involved. Make your presence felt positively by making that vital first step. Radiate a positive smile and eye contact to show others that you want to engage with them.

• People only go to sell to the room

This may be true for some people and in time, they too will learn this method only gets them so far. Experienced networkers understand the principle of "people buy from people" and that the initial interaction is about business relationship building, not selling. To avoid this pitfall, let people understand the value they can gain from your service or product after you have had that all-important thing called CONVERSATION. Ask questions about your fellow networker, instead of making it all about ME, ME,

ME. People engage better when you come across as genuinely interested. Although you are at the centre of all your networking, it does not need to be all about you.

- **Networking results are instantaneous**

Wrong. It takes a while to build those business relationships. There are some old sayings that my father used to tell me such as "short cuts do not make it" and "it is never too late for a shower of rain". This, in essence, means that things do not happen instantaneously. It takes time, but it surely will come to you if you are patient. As I say, there is a reason, time and season for everything and if you are patient it will become clear. The same can be said about networking, the right opportunity will come at the right time if you take your time and nurture relationships.

- **Either you are a natural at networking or you are not**

It is a case of adapting to your environment and around the people in the room. This is a real skill and tests your observation techniques. Invest in yourself and pursue some public speaking workshops and this will help break that initial fear or reluctance. Some people doubt their contribution to networking and feel they do not know enough people in varied fields to successfully refer people. People wonder how they can trust someone they don't really know to give them a stand-out referral or a quality referral or to recommend them to a contact. The point is you need to get to know them first before you put your reputation on the line.

- **If you see the same people in the room time and time again they are no use to you**

Seeing the same people gives you the opportunity to strengthen your relationship and subconsciously familiarise them with what it is you do, how you do it, how you can deliver it, and your USP

(Unique Selling Point); what is it that makes you stand out? You are creating a mini virtual sales team with regular attendees. Again, it's about mindset and finding positive opportunities as opposed to the perceived negatives. Not enough people in the room might translate into a poor networking session, but there could be more quality in the room. Bear in mind that you will also get extra time to have real precise interactions with the people in the room. You can have the opportunity to be specific about who you are looking for and your ideal referral.

- **You will spend more time on networking than on your own business**

This is an individual's choice and it is imperative that you weigh up the pros and cons and create a time management versus cost plan to highlight your return on investment.

- **If you own a successful business you do not need to network**

Some of the most successful people in the world see that any interaction is networking and not just reserved for an actual networking organised meeting.

Be prepared to receive a referral

As strange as it may seem, many people are not prepared to receive a referral because they focus so much time and energy into trying to secure a referral that they don't have a plan of action in place for when they eventually secure one. It is true that some referrals are more credible than others. Those that are simply a telephone or email address passed to you without personally informing the other unaware person that their details have been passed over are considered a lead and not a referral. It becomes a referral when the person whose details you received has been informed ahead of time and they have agreed to engagement. The other type of referral is a guaranteed business generation referral where it is established that, based on the recommendation, they will utilise the services of the referral.

When you receive that all important referral, regardless of the type, you must assign a plan of action against it. This can be done in many ways such as creating a spreadsheet and inputting the data which prompts you to make initial and follow up contact with dated notes to remind you what stage you're at with this particular referral.

Another method is to immediately connect and create a diarised meeting to discuss the details further. You could also have prepared templates introducing yourself and linking back to the original referral explaining why you are communicating with them and that you would like to follow up with them at their convenience. At the same time, you will provide them with dates and times to choose from to make the scheduling of diaries smoother and quicker.

Never leave that referral sitting around without ever following up on it. If you do, it will negate the effort you've spent on network marketing

Say thank you

People would like acknowledgment of the connection they have introduced to you. They appreciate courtesy such as an update or simply a 'thank you'. Be known for being appreciative as this goes a very long way. Write a testimonial for your contact or go that one step further and provide a video testimonial. This will help both of you as you'll need to state your company name at the beginning of the video and this will stay in circulation for a very long time. Think about it, it works as free advertising for your business.

A little gratitude goes a long way in establishing and maintaining your networking connection. Saying *thank you* is sometimes very much overlooked and the lack of this simple action can sabotage all your hard work. It is imperative to realise that this is also a part of the holistic networking funnel because once you establish a networking connection and they engage with you and qualify you by referring you to others, the next natural progression is to continue the engagement that leads to you both being referral partners. However, if you show a lack of gratitude, this will inevitably breakdown the relationship you have worked so hard to create.

Take those easy words and use them whether it is through your actions or verbally. Trust me when I tell you this, it is one of the easiest ways to retain a mutual networking relationship and, in turn, the rewards that you get are loyalty and free marketing by way of the response to your gratitude. When associates talk about you in a positive manner to others, this is actual marketing and it is important for you to remember this with every interaction that you have.

A lot of people feel that marketing stops at just advertising your service or product, however, you are also advertising yourself when you enter the world of networking. This small mindset adjustment will have you seeing networking in a whole new perspective. When you realise you are also part of your marketing, you will approach every interaction very differently as you will now be mindful of how you do things and how you physically come across.

Networking balance

A common problem people tend to have is trying to achieve the perfect balance between business networking and social networking. I have seen the network 'crash and burn' syndrome where someone leaves a group and either does not contact any of that group's connections again or the group does not maintain a connection with that individual. If you manage to obtain the right balance between business and social, this should not happen.

It is all down to the way you look at networking, the way you behave within that group and the relationships you form once you become a part of one. The fundamental lesson to remember is that sincerity creates an amazing relationship foundation which is hard to shatter whether you remain in a group or not. If both parties value as well as display sincerity, reliability and common goals, the relationship will continue to build upon this strong foundation no matter where your networking journey takes you.

Some people presume that because it is business networking, they must be uptight and deadly serious, but this can be off-putting as well as make others feel you are out of their league or simply unapproachable or hard to do business with. Please do not confuse being deadly serious with exuding professionalism. A professional person will adapt to their environment to make the other person comfortable within their surroundings. Some people say that there is no room for friends in business. I would say that it is all dependent on the person and their disposition as people naturally gravitate to certain personalities. Not all the people who you meet whilst networking need to automatically become your best friends and you don't need to go out of your way to achieve this. You must have a level of respect for your fellow networkers because they have a common goal with yourself, which is to get the best out of networking.

I have made some great friends, valued acquaintances, supportive referral partners or simply met great people. You choose how you want to continue the relationship, but be mindful of other people's reasons for wanting to take the business relationship forward to a "businal" (business and personal/social) level. Allow the person's actions to speak for themselves before you decide.

If someone says they are going to get back to you and they don't, this is a red flag that should alert you to be cautious and not get too close to this person. They have expressed their unreliability. If someone promises you something and they do not come through with it, then I would say be mindful and do not allow them to continue giving you false hope or letting you down. On the other hand, if someone initiates further contact, this shows their commitment and respect level to you as an individual and this shows their intention as actions speak louder than words.

Being a smiling assassin

There are times when you will feel that you are not in the mood for small talk or even not in the mood to go out and meet people whether new prospects or existing connections. The one thing to remember is that you are not alone and the characteristics and behaviours you may portray may be the same or similar as others. You must remember to push through any negative thoughts as they can be temporary, whereas the impression you leave behind could be lasting. I call this art of smiling through any mood as being the "smiling assassin". It is not something sinister, instead it is creating a positive state of mind so that no matter the situation or scenario, you smile through it and you are perceived as a positive individual come rain or shine.

This can only have positive effects on the way you are remembered by others and ultimately, marketed by others as they will always have that pleasant image of you to relay. It is very useful to be able to smile through as many *faux pas* made by yourself or others. The more you do this, the more natural it will become. Being a smiling assassin is a way to come across as objective. You'll find that people will gravitate more to this endearing characteristic.

At the same time, be wary of those who constantly smile at you and do not change their facial expressions even slightly. If you find this to be the case, quickly address whether the conversation has lost its momentum and try and reel it back to where you were able to see genuine interest from the other party.

Now that you know that the "smiling assassin" exists within all of us, you may engage slightly differently within conversations and be more aware of your impact and how others perceive you. Being aware of how people view your conversation or your demeanour is vital within the world of networking as this could be the defining factor that encourages someone to refer you and your business or not.

There have been a few times whilst I've been at a networking meeting and involved in a deep conversation with a fellow networker talking about a positive referral and setting up the next stage, when my conversation had been interrupted, giving rise to my "smiling assassin".

The interrupter, in most cases, persisted on continuing their new conversation, omitting myself, but I choose to let the "smiling assassin" win through because the original person I was talking to probably was silently analysing how I handled the situation.

The lesson here is that you must *always* be aware of how you come across verbally as well as non-verbally and a killer smile deters the negativity away from any awkward situation.

To business card or not to business card?

This has been a hot topic of conversation within many networking meet ups. Some people say that now with the art of modern technology all you have to do is send an electronic business card. Some say that they would rather take a picture of a card and they have a programme that stores the business card details. Surprisingly, in my experience, many professionals do not have a business card or if they do, a minority of them will have the wrong details imprinted on them. Or their details will be on questionably thin paper with graphics that look homemade. Be in the "elite card club" and present a card that represents who you are and what you are trying to portray. If you want to portray quality only, hand over a business card, which is considered in design and information to reflect your brand. If created in the right way the business card could become your opening topic of conversation, one that breaks the ice as well as helps steer the direction of the conversation towards your business offering. So, do you do away with the business card or not? Is there still a place for the business card or not?

Let's start with looking at the creation of your business card; it is important to have standard details on the card. As surprising as it sounds, I have seen business cards without a person's name added. Now, there is a difference between keeping it simple and lacking vital information. However, it is up to you if you keep it simple or try and cram as much information on the card as possible, but hopefully you create your ideal balance that makes it easier and more inviting for someone to get in touch at a later date. Marketeers would argue that if you have a strong brand you need to keep your business card as simple as possible as the logo will speak for itself. It might sound daft, but I have seen business cards where the telephone number has been omitted and this is a fundamental error. Without a call to action path, how do you expect someone to get in touch with you if they would like to do business with you? You may argue that there is a website address on there, but why would someone want to have to jump online to go to your website to search for your telephone number? This oversight will most probably have the recipient thinking that you have not paid any attention to this detail or do not want them to contact you. This oversight, wrongly or rightly, reflects on you as a person and although you may see this as a small detail, it is not until you are the person in receipt of such a card that you will really understand. You want to pick up the phone to speak to the person that handed the card to you and I guarantee you will be perplexed as to why this was omitted. OPPORTUNITY LOST!!!

I would suggest that if nothing else, input the basics at least on your business card including your name, position held, email address, company name/logo, telephone number, and website address if you have one.

I know many people who do not accept business cards, but instead, whilst they are conversing, connect with that individual using their LinkedIn, Twitter or Facebook account. This is great if you want to ensure you have their details there and then. The only drawback with this is you generally don't get their email address or telephone number unless they have filled in their profile details and then again if they have made their contact information visible.

With this method, if all correspondence is via the social media platform, the messages could get lost amongst the many messages you receive and does not provide the element of professionalism an email can portray. The only way to ensure you get all the details is to store everything in your phone under a new contact, but this can be time consuming and impractical if you are in a networking meeting with a lot of people.

Some people need the tangible visual business card to jog their memory of the interaction and many write information on the business cards that will help them recollect the connection. At least your business card offers a second and maybe further opportunities to be in front of that person in your absence.

If someone goes to the trouble of giving you a business card, use it to follow up and ensure you stand out from the crowd. Many people are guilty of having a business card graveyard in their handbags, briefcases, suit jackets, coat pockets, car, etc. If this is you, gather all your business cards up and create a business card spreadsheet. Delegate the job to your secretary or your virtual assistant or simply do it yourself. Do not, however, use this as an automatic spam list as you will be undoing all the hard work you have created in establishing your connections.

Another method is to find an app that you can use to take pictures of the business cards and collate them into a workable file for ease of indexing and retrieval of data.

Whether you deem the business card necessary or not, remember to have the basics on yours as this is a vehicle to return people to you. Store the details of others for ease of access for future use and remember to follow up.

- Make sure anything you send them is specific to them and not generic.

- The key sweet spot is to keep your connections updated, not victims of advertisement.

- Keep the exchange informational, let them feel you are sending them correspondence to solve an issue they may have or do not know that they have.

- Become relatable with the tone of the correspondence in terms of being conversational and personable.

- Use the other person's first name several times when addressing them.

- Give them a subtle call to action. A subtle call to action is, "if you would like to know how, read on", or "if you have experienced this then be sure to check out my blog article", and provide them with a link to follow.

CHAPTER 6: MODERN TECHNOLOGY AS THE EXTENDED NETWORKING ARENA

I have said it before that networking is not limited to a meeting but is all around us, especially in the form of social media. Love it or hate it, social media can be a minefield of potential connections. You need a clear vision and strategy for what your social media plan will be.

Networking online

Here are a few areas to consider when networking online.

- Review and identify your current social media activity.
- Structure interaction methods and strategies for implementation.
- Provide a consistent message, hook and/or theme when posting.
- Build confidence in the use of social media by being conversational and personable *en masse*.
- Understand the importance and relevancy of social media in line with your business.
- Create a clear, recurring defined message and profile to input in these platforms.
- To schedule or not to schedule or a mixture of both.

- The possibilities of outsourcing some or all of your social media.
- Learn how social media helps brand building and differentiation.
- Understand how social media can promote your content and then implement it.
- Use social media to keep your audience engaged.
- Learn how to create visibility, increase interest and generate paying customers.
- Know how to listen and respond to any online conversation that is relevant to your business goals.
- Take your brand's voice online and know which time saving tools to use to engage individuals on a daily basis.
- Avoid back-biting or taking posts and comments personally.
- Know what to post, when to post and what tone needs to be used.
- Know how to save time using online dashboards.
- Know how to communicate across different networks.
- Understand that, "If you can't tell it, you can't sell it".
- Understand which social media platform to use based on a specific target audience.
- Understand how SEO (search engine optimization) ranking has changed through Google.
- Understand how to use tools to analyse data for a marketing campaign and implement Key Performance Indicators (KPI).

Ultimately, your success with social media depends on how you use it. If it forms part of your traditional networking, it should be used to build, engage, inform, and nurture existing as well as new connections. With the increasingly popular use of video conferences and the many networking groups online, it has never been easier to network from your office or the comfort of your home and be equally or more successful. With this method you have instant access to not only your local area, but a worldwide network. It's just a key tap away.

Having said that, one of the keys to success using social media is being consistent. If you decide to use it to promote your networking, you must follow through and stay on top of all messages. Furthermore, you must be able to promote your brand in a few words, keeping the message fresh.

Knowing that you pretty much have the world as your oyster, approach your online activity very carefully as once you send it out into cyber space you cannot retract it. Be sure about the content you post, whether words or images, as this can be used to substantiate your message both negatively and positively.

I was a casualty of this once. I posted in my private page, but the information was shared outside of my network without my knowledge. Sadly, I became the centre of a Facebook media scandal. At the time, I was in my home in England and I received a telephone call to say my father had been stabbed. I could not get through to other relatives on the telephone so I decided to let my worldwide family members know in one hit online that my father had been injured. I didn't know anything for certain until I went to Facebook and saw a news article from OGNR (On the Ground News Report) with a picture of my holiday home in Jamaica and a picture of my father. The headline read, "59-year-old man stabbed to death" with his name in the content.

What were the chances of this happening? I still, to this day, am baffled as I have never seen OGNR before and have never come across it again since. What a way to find out that my father had been murdered. I went into autopilot and started typing the words "my father has been murdered in Jamaica this morning". As I used the word "Jamaica" in the sentence, the Jamaica Tourist Board suspended me for bringing "disrepute" to Jamaica. And when I returned to England heavily pregnant and with my father's body, I was declined my request for annual leave to grieve.

After a two-year relentless battle, I won my employment tribunal case on all counts against the Jamaica Tourist Board. As it is now in the public domain, I am free to talk about it, and although I make reference to it, I never disclose the full story of the horrendous time this was. It can be easily found in the employment tribunal records if anyone ever wanted to know everything.

I shall be releasing my book around this tumultuous time in the middle of next year which will detail cover ups, death threats, adversity, trauma and things that would make the hardened person's stomach churn. It is important for me to share an overview of my story as this is why I started my company, *Training Personified*, due to the inhumane way in which I had been treated by my previous employer whilst this all went on.

Training Personified initially focused on relaying the ideology that customer service is key to the success of any given organisation and that internal customers (employees) are just as important as external customers. If you look after the internal customers, your external customers will be looked after as a matter of natural progression. With the sharing of my story within networking, my company direction has gained more avenues. As I now deliver public speaking workshops, I have become a Multi Award Winning International Speaker and keynote at a number of confidence building workshops.

If social media is the only route you are using to network, you will be using it to create relationships and you will need a strategy to push your message forward. Firstly, you need to establish whether it is visibility you are after or a direct audience that can potentially turn into clients or marketeers or both. Whatever your motive, create a plan around it with the idea to yield positive results. Surprisingly, the high amount of online profiles that have little or no information is astounding. This is an opportunity (or many) lost over a period; people must be able to obtain information about you and find a way to contact you via email, website or telephone.

You need to describe who you are, what you do, how you do it, what problem, if any, do you solve, and the value you provide. And any information you input should be current.

Keep it relevant to both your business and your market. You can't market to everyone, so don't try. In this information age, people are often overloaded with data, so keep your message on the shorter side. For Twitter, it should be a very brief current message, perhaps your next appearance, schedule updates or any new changes to your company that are of interest to the public. For example, a designer might announce a new clothing line. For larger venues such as Facebook, keep it to one or two paragraphs unless you're writing a blog. If that's the case, break the message up with bullets and/or subheadings so the reader doesn't get bored. People tend to scan when they read 'information'.

It should reflect you and your personality as, after all, you want to translate yourself as genuine and as real as possible. You want your image to imitate the 'real life' you enjoy. This will allow people to feel like they know you better and they will begin to trust you. Your credibility will grow if you're consistent.

It is important to note that you do not necessarily need a website, but you need something that takes people to a place where they can find out more information such as a social media page, a landing page or a directory page, etc. Visibility on its own does not pay the bills; the plan for social media networking needs to be similar to the face-to-face networking and ultimately it needs to be a plan to create new engagement or retain existing connections that are interested enough to invest in you in one way or another whether that be time, money, engagement, or further promoting what you do by sharing your visibility with their connections. The latter is described as *network expansion*. You should be aiming for the ideology that vanity is ineffective alone without a *call to action*, and profit is the reality you want to create and sustain through considered measures.

A call to action is an instructional prompter that encourages your audience to engage further. You can use a telephone number saying, "Call now" or an informational prompter to "Click here". It is a way of getting your prospect to act using your instructional guide. Face-to-face networking also benefits a lot more with a call to action and you can subtly use this with props such as a roller banner, your business card, flyers, leaflets, or your elevator pitch.

Social media engagement is not only about building your network but generating leads that you ultimately turn into conversion over time. It is important to be patient with social media as you must not forget the 'social' element within the name and there is a need to nurture it effectively, progressively.

How to choose your groups and budget your networking

- Choosing the right group
- To pay or not to pay
- Membership

- Flexibility
- What structure does it offer?
- Location
- Similar or different trades
- Atmosphere
- Growth
- Values
- Member benefits
- Frequency of group

There once was a time when most networking groups that existed were via paid membership plus meet fee attendance costs. There has now been an influx of free networking meetings and it is best to analyse the above before handing over your money. The emergence of many free networking groups has made it easier for those on a tight budget or those who need to justify membership fees even though they can engage with many more people than they once had networking access to. I am not against paid meeting memberships or meet fees as long as the membership you are paying for provides value for what they are offering.

Ask yourself what they are offering that is more than what the free networking opportunity is giving you. Does the scheduled meeting fit around your lifestyle? Membership groups that do not hold you to one location but allow you to attend different locations to help you expand your network are very beneficial.

Prepare yourself when networking

When you are out and about, listen for signs when you are either directly or indirectly in a conversation such as:

TOP TIP ALERT

THERE IS ALWAYS A NETWORKING OPPORTUNITY if you listen hard enough for it.

DO NOT wait until you are in a room to "Network"

THERE IS NEVER AN EXCUSE THAT YOU ARE TOO BUSY TO NETWORK... There are family, friends, neighbours, people you see in supermarkets, etc.

When out and about – **Listen for OPENERS**

Use your **social media network**

Connect businesses you may engage with but only those **you trust** with credibility

PREPARE YOUR NETWORKING INTRO'S SENTENCE TO INTRODUCE YOURSELF ON A ONE-TO-ONE BASIS

_____

_____

_____

_____

_____

_____

_____

_____

WRITE A SENTENCE TO INTRODUCE YOURSELF TO TWO OR MORE PEOPLE CONVERSING

_____

_____

_____

_____

_____

_____

_____

CREATE A QUESTION TO FIND OUT MORE ABOUT SOMEONE

_____

_____

_____

_____

_____

Conversation saver questions

WRITE THREE QUESTIONS TO CREATE FOLLOW-UPS

1. _____

_____

2. _____

_____

3. _____

_____

CREATE TWO SENTENCES TO INTRODUCE OTHERS

1._____

_____

_____

2._____

_____

_____

A SENTENCE TO DESCRIBE WHAT YOU DO

1._____

_____

_____

_____

_____

_____

_____

_____

Develop a thick skin

There will be times when people may say things that you do not like and you'll need to learn to walk away from it and not take it personally. What is important to you may not even be worth considering for the other person; their intention may not be anything to do with you, especially in a detrimental light. The easiest way to resolve this is to just keep being uniquely you and simply "Do You". Focus on your task at hand and pursue that end goal without rushing and bulldozing your way along. Take a moment, analyse what is going on and decide how you are going to achieve your final mission. However, at the same time, you have to take heed of the overall journey and the way in which you learn; absorb and utilise interactions and the lessons learned on the way. This will add weight to the end result.

Networking has moved forward; not only is it just face-to-face now but it exists online too. Far too many people get caught up in the words that are written on the screen as we feel that because we are reading them they have something to do with us and we must internalise the words or dissect them to make sense. The simple truth is that it is none of our business unless a post has specifically mentioned our names.

The one thing to remember is that we can choose to make the words we receive 'powerful' or we can choose to let them be water off a duck's back. In many cases, the person writing is looking for a reaction, but the receiver will read it and come to their own conclusions and this can cause all sorts of problems for you. The pivotal point to remember when reading or responding is *do your responses and thoughts reflect upon your personal branding*? If the answer is no then step away from the situation and go and do one of your items on your to-do list away from social media. You'll find that once-important comment has now become less significant as you are doing something to satisfy your goal.

- Follow up and build rapport.
- Connect with people on a 'no strings attached' basis
- Make time to follow up for 30 minutes minimum a day.

Build rapport

Rapport exists when two people develop a feeling of harmony, well-being and security. It can be compared to musical resonance. When you strike a note on a tuning fork and hold it near to another tuning fork, the second will also start to vibrate even though they do not touch. This resonance or rapport occurs between people when they work and live in an open, trusting and contented relationship.

It is pointless to build up a network and then not utilise or connect with it, or connect its members with other relevant contacts. The value is within the circle; who you know. You have no initial idea of the impact a contact can have for you beyond who you can visibly see in front of you. You can't know what opportunities could arise from knowing a particular person. Spending the time to build up a network is time you could have spent elsewhere on your business, so it is important not to waste the hard work you have built up gathering your network so far.

The person you need to connect to right now might be a mutual connection's neighbour, family member, business associate, etc. As I've mentioned earlier in this book, don't be dismissive of any connection, especially if you initially feel they are not able to assist you on a business networking journey. This is supported by Frigyes Karinthy in 1929 where he describes "*six degrees of separation*" as the idea that all living things in the world are six or fewer steps away from each other through the chain of a friend of a friend.

Build positive relationships

Rapport is about meeting people on their own level and making them feel at ease. It is based on mutual respect and agreement.

When you relate to other people you can choose one of two standpoints from which to start:

You can concentrate on the differences between you.
Or
You can emphasise the similarities between you (the things you agree on, feel and think the same about and react the same way to).

If you emphasise the differences, it will be virtually impossible to develop a rapport.

The emphasis on similarities and/or differences occur not just in the words we use when talking to others, but in the way we express ourselves through tone, body language and attitude.

For example, if one person is standing talking loudly, the result will be to emphasise the differences between them and someone who is sitting and talking quietly, even if they are saying the same things.

Matching or mirroring is an effective tool for building rapport. It is a way of holding up a mirror to another person so that they see a reflection of their own actions and statements through your physical posture and gestures.

Body language

When you are in rapport with another person, your body language will naturally tend to mirror the other person's. When you are trying to establish rapport with another person, consider whether your body language is 'jarring' with theirs. Consider for example:

- Sitting position
- Movement and position of legs and arms
- Overall posture

- Walk
- Dress
- Facial expression
- Breathing
- Speech

Similarly, we need to be aware of our speech and consider whether this is contributing to rapport. Consider your use of:

- Pitch
- Tone
- Volume
- Choice of words
- Jargon
- Slang
- Professional terms

Reflection

You can build rapport by initially reflecting the same feelings and moods as the other person, or at least demonstrating an appreciation of how they are feeling – particularly when those feelings are positive. Even where those feelings are negative, for example, the other person is tense and angry, you will need to acknowledge and respect this to build rapport and move the conversation forward constructively.

In any discussion, it is paramount to show respect for the other person's skills, qualities, experience, beliefs, and feelings whether we agree with them or not.

TOP TIP ALERT

When networking, look beyond a person's job title as they may have alternative skills that would align with your ideal connection or referral. I have seen people dismiss having a 1-to-1 with someone because of the job they do, but they have no idea what other skill sets that person may possess, who they may know beyond the room and if they have anything in common to create a possible synergy. Do not assume that there may be nothing that other person can offer you based on what you perceive, preconceive or via the partial glimpse you're exposed to.

Eight key factors to building loyalty

People don't have to engage with you and they don't have to tell their friends how great your business is. However, if you put in the effort to earn their loyalty, that's exactly what they'll do.

An ongoing challenge for any company is the retention of customers. Incorporating these eight ingredients to a well-rounded strategy for building loyalty will produce remarkable results.

1. Be Reliable: Reliability arises from consistent follow-through and execution. Turn up for a meeting on time. Deliver what you have committed to in a timely manner.

2. Be Credible: Credibility is enhanced when you do exactly what you say you will do, every time. Avoid holding any hidden agenda. Exude value in your product or service offering.

3. Be Responsive: Share your counterpart's sense of urgency. Be accessible and approachable as much as possible. Give examples of you being able to deliver results by openly allowing others to see feedback and testimonials about you or your business.

4. Show Empathy: Assess the individual's emotions and show compassion. If someone seems anxious, reassure them. If someone is excited, share that excitement through comments, voice and other nonverbal messages. Use their own terms to reinforce feelings.

5. Be Friendly: Whilst networking, always remember to smile. Do not bring your problems with you whilst networking. Approach individuals and do not wait for them to come to you. Move around and introduce yourself to as many different people as possible.

6. Be Accessible: Allow individuals to connect with you easily following your initial interaction. Do not give them follow up contact details that places them in front of the 'gatekeeper' (the person that controls if you get through or not to the intended person you want to speak to). Also do not provide details that you do not respond to as this will negatively impact on your reliability.

Chapter 7: Make Networking Work for You

When it comes to networking you'll need to be innovative about how you make it work for you, how you fit it into your normal day to day activities and make it convenient for you.

Combine networking with scheduled meetings

One way to help with your time management is to schedule out which networking meetings you will be attending and add them to your diary. When you are setting face-to-face meetings with people, combine it with one of the networking meetings that you will be attending. This frees up your time and enables a multitude of possible responses from the receiver, such as:

- You are that busy that you need to blend it with an existing activity.
- They can see your 'net-worth' by the number of people you know at the networking meeting.

You can also use this opportunity to introduce them to other people with whom they may create a mutually beneficial business relationship.

Once you get into the habit of doing this, you will notice that your schedule becomes slicker and you'll know that networking will most definitely work for you as you are blending it with other valuable activities. People tend to look for ways to hone their time management, so bear in mind that this is the ideal way. This method also works very well for those individuals who work from home and do not have an open office to the public or clients. This way you can utilise the networking venue's premises without the need to look for hiring spaces or locating a meet-up spot purely for meetings. We are now in an age where working from home is more convenient and cost effective and as such, you must look at innovative methods to make it work for you. Structuring your networking in the right way can massively assist with this.

Let your passion shine

Why, oh, why do I still see people with sullen faces when they are networking? Do they want to give off the wrong initial impression?

Let the passion ooze out of you for your product, service or skill set. If you believe and exude that you love what you do and what you stand for, then others will also buy into it. If you are not passionate about what you want, then how on earth can you expect your audience to engage with the concept as well? Don't be afraid to let your personality come out. Remember, people do business with people. If you are 'one of many of the same' profession who is in the room, what is going to make you stand out over the rest? What is your USP (unique selling point)? Why should someone pass a referral to you over the others in the room who are doing similar things? You must ask yourself these questions and be ready to answer them.

Share your testimonial stories with people, especially when you are delivering your elevator pitch. Let people see how others have engaged with your offering by providing them with a brief list of your past clients and what your positive value was towards them. The key word is VALUE, as in, *what value do you offer and can you back it up with evidence*? Now, the way in which you present this information will make all the difference, if you say it in a non-committal way with zero passion it will be harder to believe in what you are saying. However, if the passion exudes from within you then it will encourage your audience to trust in you and what you are saying.

There are times when you may not feel on top of your game and you will struggle to let the passion shine, but remind yourself to get over it, pull yourself together and do what is necessary to achieve your ultimate goal of generating business through positive business relationship building. There will be days when you'll feel overwhelmed with the many things that you have to do in your day to day schedule, and networking might feel like another of those tasks, but you have to remember that there are always going to be networking opportunities and you don't have to chase every single one down, especially if you are not in the right frame of mind. Wait until you feel ready.

But if you are one of those people who feels nervous when it comes to networking, then **work on it**. The simplest way to do this is to prepare by using the introduction questions mentioned earlier in this book. During the time when you are not feeling 100%, do not push yourself to attend a meeting; wait until you are in top form. Otherwise you will be doing yourself a disservice. The last thing you need is to have people thinking that this is the way you conduct your business.

Remember that networking gets better with practice; the more you attend, the more comfortable you will begin to feel. Your aim is to be the best representation of yourself, brand, service, product, and skill-sets.

Smile; it is easy and costs nothing. If you struggle with smiling, then face that mirror of yours and practice, practice, practice. A simple smile opens the doors to many opportunities; you'll thank me for this advice later.

If you don't take the leap of faith and step out of your comfort zone, you will never know what could have been. Take the networking 'risk' and look forward to finding out exactly where it will lead you. The worst that can happen is that you do not make any connections that lead to business, but then you are no worse off than when you first started. All you will have gained are some networking connections, even if it's without the certainty of a monetary reward; the point is that you now have new connections. These connections may open exciting doors of possibilities that, in the future, may direct you towards a lead that you've always wanted. All you have to do is trust in yourself and your unique potential.

Look for the opportunities that each networking group has to offer and make the most out of the ones that are most beneficial for you and your business.

The lesson here is to be prepared; be prepared to talk to as many people as possible; be prepared to stand up and deliver a heartfelt stand-out pitch; be prepared to answer questions about your field of expertise and be prepared to follow up.

Your overall commitment will define exactly how networking works for you.

Now that you have the knowledge of networking, it is ultimately about mindset; give it a whirl and let me know how you get on by leaving your feedback on *www.motivationalqueen.com* or creating a video testimonial. I will happily upload it on my digital media platforms. You can send details via the **contact us** link on my website.

Remember to fill this in again once you have applied the principles outlined in this book. Place a tick in the box underneath the options that you identify with most.

	Confident	Average	Daunted	Don't know
How do you feel about networking?				
How are you at meeting new people?				
How are you at instigating a conversation?				
How are you at delivering a pitch?				

How are you at referring others/finding referrals?				
Do you feel you can easily excel at networking?				
How do you feel about generating business?				

Create your plan of action

_____

_____

_____

_____

_____

Never
Enter
The
World
Of
Relationships
Knowledge-less
Indecisive
Needy or
Greedy

The message here is to research, know what you want and prepare and practice to ensure that you get the most out of business networking. There is also a need to be aware that networking encompasses relationships of many different spectrums and it is important to be mindful that each one needs to be nurtured with many of those having different needs. When networking, if someone ever comes across as desperate to secure a sale or deal, that 'air of neediness' will turn people off and make that person seem as if they're better off avoided. Even worse, a needy person may come across as 'greedy', or people might just feel sorry for them (but not in a healthy way). In the case of this approach, it usually creates an unfavourable reputation of the 'needy networker' and as I've already mentioned, people are each other's marketeers. It is better to leave a positive long-lasting impression.

Conclusion

The underlying message is that 'Networking is Personified.' That means networking is personal to you and your wants, requirements and needs.

Every person has a different set of circumstances and a desired outcome that they are working towards. We each have our own unique style, personal feelings towards networking and our own thought process which shapes how we perceive and assess situations.

Networking, in essence, is about being unique, about embracing an individual style and utilising set guidelines to strengthen it. By adapting the methods within this book, you will effectively work around your goals and objectives as well as understand networking through the eyes of others. Don't be afraid to be unorthodox in your approach as ultimately this will make you stand out from the crowd. In the midst of your tailored approach, be sure to ask yourself the following questions.

- How will people receive this?
- How will people perceive this?
- Am I being concise?
- Am I being precise?
- Do people understand the value I provide?
- Have I made it easy for people to get in touch with me if I am not physically present?

Having considered all the above and the content within this book, you will have hopefully obtained a more holistic understanding of networking, enabling you to create a plan of action. The key, however, is not only to have the plan but to **action** by implementation. Not 'could have', 'should have' or 'would have', but ACTION today.

- Assess
- Research
- Plan
- Implement

Use this book and dip into it from time to time as it will guide you through the whimsical yet wonderful world of networking. It will, no doubt, yield a whole host of opportunities and life-changing directions with the people you meet, the experiences you encounter and the transformative memories you make.

GOOD LUCK!

ABOUT THE AUTHOR

Zoe Bennett MA, aka Motivational Queen™, is an International Motivational Speaker who blends both business and personal development together. She specialises in helping others succeed through overwhelming adversity using mindset to find inner motivation, strength, strategy and drive to ensure success.

She has a Masters Degree in Tourism Management and has previously worked within the tourism industry for 16 years. While living in the UK (United Kingdom), she worked for the Jamaican government promoting that country to the UK market. In her first few months in this post, she was nominated for the 2005 TTG Supplier Sales Agent of the Year.

When her father was brutally murdered in Jamaica, she mentioned it on Facebook and subsequently became involved in a two-year legal battle with the Jamaica Tourist Board who suspended her at a time when she was transporting her father's deceased body back to the UK. After a long legal battle, Zoe eventually won the case.

After her father's killer's trial was postponed seven times, she relentlessly pursued justice. Through persevering, sheer grit, determination and her 'never give up' attitude, it paid off when the murderer was convicted to 40 years to life without parole.

Statistics published by LEP (Lancashire Evening Post), 20th March 2014 tell us, "The conviction rate for murder in Jamaica is 5%." This conviction was considered a huge success and was written about in the U.K national newspapers and magazines.

Zoe also draws upon her own experience as a victim of a brutal rape (the perpetrator served just three years in jail) to provide confidence building workshops to women from disadvantaged backgrounds, victims of DV (domestic violence), FGM (Female Genital Mutilation) and honour-based violence. She also owns a corporate personal development training company, Training Personified Ltd that specialises in interpersonal skills, focusing on being fun, interactive, engaging, practicing cooperation within the team, and exceeding the customer's expectation.

Through her life story, many learn strategies and insights into how to breed success through adversity as well as how to network for success. Zoe is a passionate and an incredible people person who is always looking for ways to help people and causes dear to her heart. She is described as "inspirational", "motivational", "a strong and confident individual", "fun, energetic and inspirational". Her energy on stage is infectious and never fails to engage the audience. Her ultimate message is "never give up!"

She is now coined The Motivational Queen and delivers talks to schools, FTSE100 companies and apprentices where they receive resilience, entrepreneurship and employability skills training all blended with Zoe's inspirational life lessons.

Her Awards and Credentials Include:

- Delivering partner for the charity *Seek for Change*
- Sits on the Birmingham Business Board for the *NSPCC* (National Society For The Prevention of Cruelty To Children)
- Ambassador for *The Women and Families Resource Centre* and a champion for *Include Me* Too.
- Speaking at conferences in India, Netherlands and many events throughout the UK.
- Founder of the *MBCC Awards* (Midlands Business and Community Charity Awards), a platform for unsung heroes, which gives all profits to recipient charities *www.midlandsbccawards.co.uk*
- Founder of the *Removing the Shame and Guilt Conference* for women who suffer physical violence. She has subsequently created a similar program for men.
- May 2017 *WEF* (Women's Economic Forum) *Iconic Woman Creating a Better World for Others*, New Delhi, India
- June 2017 "Inspirational Woman of the Year" by *Powerhouse Global*
- Awarded 2017 "Outstanding Diva" at the *Divas of Colour Awards*
- 2016 "Most Influential Business Woman" from *Acquisition International*, West Midlands

- Awarded "Human Excellency Award" from *United Nations Mission of International Relations*
- Awarded "Career Woman of the Year" by A*ll Women Achievers Awards*
- 2016 "Inspirational Speaker of the Year" from *Women of Purpose Awards*
- Winner of West Midlands "Woman of the Year" and "Inspirational Woman of the Year"
- Featured in the *Daily Mail, The Mirror, BBC* (British Broadcasting Channel) *Radio, Lancashire Evening Post, Love It,* and *Pick Me Up* magazine

References and Resources

1. https://www.youtube.com/watch?v=9klQDHgCrE8&sns=tw

2. http://www.dailymail.co.uk/news/article-2779579/British-marketing-rep-sacked-Jamaican-Tourist-Board-Facebook-outburst-father-s-machete-murder-island-wins-case-unfair-dismissal.html

3. https://www.change.org/p/please-help-us-ask-david-cameron-to-help-get-justice-for-our-brutally-murdered- dad

4. https://www.osac.gov/Pages/ContentReportDetails.aspx?cid=12216

5. http://www.lep.co.uk/news/local/he-was-murdered-in-the-most-barbaric-way-1-4111181

6. http://www.dailymail.co.uk/news/article-2086825/Daughter-attacked-Jamaican-fathers-killers-Facebook-suspended-countrys-tourist-board.html

7. http://www.lep.co.uk/community/local_services_2_1889/deaths-funerals-and-cremations/errol_s_grieving_girl_suspended_1_4141762

8. http://www.grumpyoldsod.com/jamaica.asp

9. http://www.grumpyoldsod.com/jamaica2.asp

10. http://books.google.co.uk/books?id=5pkZozyh4uUC&pg=
    PA180&lpg=PA180&dq=zoe+bennett+jamaica&source=bl
    &ots=Q8p2HYQWqY&sig=kIKd8bbcTvOaop7LiiCcGEV
    1VYs&hl=en&sa=X&ei=1-oOUd_ZJsLJ0QWFvIGoAw&
    ved=0CEIQ6AEwBA#v=onepage&q=zoe%20bennett%20
    jamaica&f=false

11. https://repositories.lib.utexas.edu/bitstream/handle/2152/
    ETD-UT-2012-05-5846/WINT-MASTERS-REPORT.
    pdf?sequence=1 <https://repositories.lib.utexas.edu/bitstream/
    handle/2152/ETD-UT-2012-05-5846/WINT-MASTERS-
    REPORT.pdf?sequence=1

12. https://www.facebook.com/trainingpersonified.learning/
    videos/282444948777824/

13. https://www.facebook.com/trainingpersonified.learning/
    videos/252524758436510/

14. https://www.facebook.com/trainingpersonified.learning/
    videos/288904061465246/